W… Don't K… Sex...

A Funny "Eye-Opening" Quiz

I AM SURE YOU KNOW EVERYTHING !

THIS IS TO AMUSE YOU WHEN DAD IS SLEEPING

JEN XXXX

What Boomers Don't Know about Sex...

A Funny "Eye-Opening" Quiz

Linda Knaus

Illustrated by Steve Mark

Meadowbrook Press
Distributed by Simon & Schuster
New York

Library of Congress Cataloging-in-Publication Data

Knaus, Linda, 1961-
What boomers don't know about sex-- a funny "eye-opening" quiz / by Linda Knaus.
p. cm.
ISBN: 978-0-88166-546-8 (Meadowbrook Press)
ISBN: 978-0-684-06944-9 (Simon & Schuster)
1. Baby boom generation--Humor. 2. Sex--Humor. 3. Aging--Humor. 4. Middle-aged persons--Humor. I. Title.
PN6231.B22K57 2009
818'.602--dc22

2008053424

Editor: Alicia Ester
Proofreader: Angela Wiechmann
Production Manager: Paul Woods
Graphic Design Manager: Tamara Peterson
Cover Art and Interior Illustrations: Steve Mark

Published by Meadowbrook Press
5451 Smetana Drive
Minnetonka, Minnesota 55343
www.meadowbrookpress.com

BOOK TRADE DISTRIBUTION by
Simon and Schuster, a division of Simon and Schuster, Inc.
1230 Avenue of the Americas
New York, New York 10020

13 12 11 10 09 10 9 8 7 6 5 4 3 2 1

Printed in the United States of America

Dedication

For my husband, Snorri.

Acknowledgments

For their thoughtful reviews of this book's content,
Meadowbrook Press thanks the following people:

Polly Andersen, Sabi Bagherli, Marel Conner, Larry Holgerson,
Marti Holgerson, John Jacobson, Leatte Magnan, Bethany Miller,
Helen Olson, Kathy Wollersheim, Mark Wollersheim, Paul Woods

Q: What does it mean when an older woman becomes flushed and tingly and she cries out in excitement?

A: *She's got bingo.*

Q: Do older men get out of breath during sex?

A: *Yes, but in their defense, blowing up an inflatable doll is a lot of work.*

Q: What's the fastest way for a boomer couple to get hot and bothered in the bedroom?

A: *Adjust the thermostat.*

Q: After lovemaking, a younger man may say, "How was it for you?" What's an older man likely to say?

A: *"Where's my orthopedic back pillow?"*

Q: What are three things a middle-aged man can do to arouse his wife?

A: *Vacuum, dust, mop.*

Q: What can an older couple buy to make sleeping together more pleasurable?

A: *Side-by-side recliners.*

Q: Why does an older woman want to be on top during sex?

A: *To keep her husband from getting away.*

Q: Why don't older couples have sex very often?

A: *As soon as they get to the bedroom, they can't remember why they went there.*

Q: What are two reasons boomers don't play footsie?

A: *Corns and bunions.*

Q: What's a young woman's motto?

A: *"A good man is hard to find."*

Q: What's a middle-aged woman's motto?

A: *"A hard man is good to find."*

Q: What does it mean when a middle-aged man runs his hands up and down his wife's body in bed?

A: *He's looking for the remote.*

Q: When should an older couple buy new furniture to liven up their bedroom ambiance?

A: *When he no longer notices her chest, and she stops rummaging through his drawers.*

Q: Buying condoms can be embarrassing for younger men. Is it a problem for older men?

A: *No, they get their wives to buy them.*

Q: When should boomer men take Viagra?

A: *When it's difficult to get up in the morning.*

Q: What replaces birth control issues for boomer women?

A: *Bladder control issues.*

Q: Do older couples ever drink a little bubbly to get in the mood?

A: *If you mean* Alka-Seltzer, *yes.*

Q: When does a man lose interest in sex with his wife?

A: *When she starts to look like her mother.*

Q: If you ask a young couple when they last had sex, they check their watches. What do older couples check?

A: *Their calendars.*

Q: Boomer men say they wish they could remember the last time they had sex. What do boomer women say?

A: *They wish they could forget the last time they had sex.*

Q: Is testosterone loss the only reason older men stop wanting sex?

A: *Yes—it has absolutely nothing to do with the fact that their wives are old, wrinkled, and gray.*

Q: When young people have sex, what do they worry about most?

A: *Getting caught by their parents.*

Q: When older people have sex, what do they worry about most?

A: *Getting caught by their grandchildren.*

Q: Is it acceptable for a boomer to wear garter belts and sexy stockings in the bedroom?

A: *If his wife doesn't mind, why not?*

SPORTS

Q: How does a middle-aged couple's sex life change throughout the years?

A: *When they're young, he waits patiently through her "hard-to-get" phase. When they're older, she waits patiently through his "get-to-hard" phase.*

Q: If an older man takes a sex quiz and flunks, should he tell his wife?

A: *Sure—she'll pretend to be surprised.*

Q: How can an older couple combine sex and gambling?

A: *He says, "Do you want to get lucky?" She responds, "No dice."*

Q: What's a middle-aged woman's version of hot pants?

A: *Sweatpants right out of the dryer.*

Q: What's the greatest advantage to middle-aged sex?

A: *Everything looks bigger with bifocals.*

Q: If a boomer becomes stiff, should his wife assume he's ready for sex?

A: *Either that, or rigor mortis has set in.*

Q: What's a middle-aged woman's favorite bedroom position?

A: *Her on a king-size canopy bed and him on a cot.*

Q: What do young women want their husbands to do during sex?

A: *Slow down.*

Q: What do older women want their husbands to do during sex?

A: *Hurry up.*

Q: What activity leaves boomers sweating, moaning, and breathing hard in the bedroom?

A: *Rearranging the furniture.*

Q: What's the middle age version of thongs and thigh highs?

A: *Girdles and support hose.*

Q: How does an older couple stay amused in bed?

A: *By making their mattress go up and down with the press of a button.*

Q: Why would a man take Viagra if he'll be sleeping alone?

A: *So he won't roll out of bed.*

Q: What's the difference between young men and middle-aged men?

A: *A young man wonders if he'll get laid, and a middle-aged man wonders if he'll get laid off.*

Q: Should boomer couples try new sexual positions?

A: *Not without putting the chiropractor on speed dial.*

Q: Do older people ever have sex outside?

A: *Yes, but only after consulting the Weather Channel.*

Q: What does "sex, drugs, and rock 'n' roll" mean for an older couple?

A: *He takes Viagra for sex, only to discover she's fallen asleep in the rocker with rollers in her hair.*

ZZZZZ

Q: Are older men better in bed than younger men, seeing they have so much more experience?

A: *You'd think so, wouldn't you?*

Q: Why do middle-aged couples worry so much about sex and finances?

A: *In both cases, they're afraid of losing interest.*

Q: Do boomers go out after having sex?

A: *No, but their backs do.*

Q: When does an older woman try to get into a man's pants?

A: *When her own don't fit anymore.*

Q: What do older people buy in adult novelty stores?

A: *High-fiber edible panties.*

NOW
HIGH IN FIBER
EDIBLE PANTY

Q: What's the most horrifying sexual experience an older couple can have?

A: *Catching a glimpse of themselves in the mirror on the ceiling.*

Q: How can an older woman get her husband interested in a new sex toy?

A: *By buying one that comes with a remote.*

Q: Do boomer couples have sex less often than they did when they were younger?

A: *If only they could remember.*

Q: What's a sure sign a couple is getting too old for hanky panky?

A: *They still refer to sex as "hanky panky."*

Q: Do middle-aged couples still flirt?

A: *Yes, but rarely with each other.*

WINK
WINK

Q: What's safe sex for older couples?

A: *Putting a guardrail on the bed.*

Q: What replaces the need to relieve sexual tension in older men?

A: *The need to relieve gas pressure.*

Q: What does an older woman put on when she says she'll "slip into something more comfortable"?

A: *Orthopedic shoes.*

Q: When is birth control no longer necessary?

A: *When sex is inconceivable.*

Q: When's the best time for boomer couples to make love?

A: *After the kids leave for college.*

STATE
S
U15

Q: What should a man do if he suffers from erectile dysfunction plus an enlarged prostate?

A: *Be careful not to mix up his medications.*

Q: When should a woman stop wearing her see-through nightie?

A: *When her husband can't see through it without his glasses.*

Q: What does it mean when a young woman hears a whistle?

A: *She looks hot.*

Q: What does it mean when an older woman hears a whistle?

A: *Her tea is hot.*

Q: Can an older woman keep her husband's heart healthy with frequent, rigorous sex?

A: *Either that, or she just might kill him.*

Q: Why do middle-aged men always remember their wedding anniversaries?

A: *It's the one night a year they get lucky.*

Q: What's the difference between a young woman and an older woman?

A: *A young woman wants to find a good hubby, and an older woman wants to find a good hobby.*

Q: How is boomer sex like an appendectomy?

A: *Both are major operations.*

Q: What's the hottest spot for middle-aged honeymooners?

A: *Viagra Falls.*

Q: What's the fastest way for an older woman to get rid of an obscene phone caller?

A: *Tell him what she's wearing.*

Q: Do women often laugh behind their husbands' backs?

A: *No, the funny parts are in front.*

Q: What did the boomer couple discover when they opened their box of sex toys?

A: *Cobwebs.*

Q: What happens when a woman replaces her husband's sleeping pills with Viagra?

A: *He's up all night.*

Q: Where's the best place for boomer singles to meet?

A: *The pharmacy aisle.*

Q: To an older woman, what does *kinky* refer to?

A: *The way her hair gets after a bad perm.*

Q: When does a woman suspect she's losing her sex appeal?

A: *When the clerk at the supermarket calls her "sir."*

Q: What's a good birth control method for a middle-aged couple?

A: *Seeing each other naked.*

Q: What does the term *wild oats* mean to a young man?

A: *A time to experience many sexual relationships.*

Q: What does the term *wild oats* mean to an older man?

A: *A high-fiber breakfast.*

Q: How can a husband tell his wife is becoming more religious as she ages?

A: *By how often she says, "Oh God, not tonight!"*

Q: What's the most popular brand of massage oil for the boomer crowd?

A: *Bengay.*

Q: Do older men always fall asleep after sex?

A: *Not always. Sometimes they can't hold out that long.*

zZZZZ

Q: In bed, younger women say things like, "You're driving me wild." What do older women say?

A: *"Wake up—you're drooling on me."*

Q: What does a DD bra size mean for older women?

A: *Dangerously droopy.*

Q: Why do 50-year-olds deal with heartache better than younger people?

A: *Because at that age, everything hurts.*

Q: What's the middle-aged version of oral sex?

A: *Talking about how good it used to be.*

Q: What's the best way for an older woman to discourage Peeping Toms?

A: *Leave her shades up.*

Q: If an older woman fails to arouse her husband with sexy lingerie, what should she put on?

A: *A horror movie. If she's lucky, he'll be scared stiff.*

Q: What's an older couple's favorite romantic hideaway?

A: *Whichever restaurant has the best Early Bird Special.*

Q: What's the upside to having an empty nest?

A: *No need to lock the bedroom door.*

Q: Why do older people fumble around during sex?

A: *All that heavy breathing fogs up their glasses.*

Q: If a man can't get a prescription for Viagra, is there an over-the-counter product he can use instead?

A: *Miracle-Gro.*

Q: Do older couples ever make love doggy style?

A: *Yes—he begs, and she rolls over and plays dead.*

Q: What's a hot night in bed for older couples?

A: *When the electric blanket is cranked up too high.*

Q: When should a woman worry her husband is losing interest in sex?

A: *When he switches from* Penthouse *to* Reader's Digest.

Q: How can you tell if a man is too old to call a sex hotline?

A: *He still has a rotary dial phone.*

Q: What's the leading cause of erectile dysfunction in older men?

A: *Wives who come to bed in bunny slippers, cold cream, and chocolate-syrup stained robes.*

HOME

Q: When an older couple has a candlelight dinner, what inevitably follows?

A: *An argument about who forgot to pay the electric bill.*

Q: What should boomer men be careful to avoid?

A: *Mistaking their Viagra for their stool softener.*

Q: What's a nooner for young people?

A: *Sex during the day.*

Q: What's a nooner for older people?

A: *A nap.*

Q: Why do boomers spend less time in the bedroom than they used to?

A: *Because they spend more time in the bathroom than they used to.*

Q: Should a man see a doctor if he can't stand going to bed with the same annoying pain?

A: *No, a divorce attorney would get rid of the pain a lot quicker.*

Q: At what point should an older couple just give up on sex?

A: *When they're* both *faking it.*

Oh my God.
Oh my God.

Also from Meadowbrook Press

What You Don't Know about Turning 40... This over-the-hill birthday gift is a pop quiz sure to liven up any 40th birthday party. The book is adorned with cartoons by Steve Mark that make it fun to read even after the party has ended.

What You Don't Know about Turning 50... This funny birthday quiz contains outrageous answers to commonly asked questions about turning 50. This book contains everything you always wanted to know about the big five-o.

What You Don't Know about Turning 60... Q: What's a senior screwdriver? A: Orange juice and Metamucil. This hilarious pop quiz eases the pain of turning 60, provides entertainment for over-the-hill birthday parties, and is fun to read when reality sets in.

What Women Don't Know about Getting Older... is a funny quiz with 100 questions that will have you roaring with laughter about "life changes" and all its ups and downs. This book is the perfect gift for any middle-aged woman—and anyone who needs a good laugh!.